Awaken the Soul

Self-Awareness

Hattie Spiritweaver

CONTENTS

ACKNOWLEDGMENTS

There are many people to thank on this awesome journey called life. I've had many great mentors and met various people along the way who contributed to my path of success.

Each one of them played a role and part in encouraging me to become my best authentic self. I appreciate every one of you, and there are too many to account around the globe. You all know who you are, and whether it was big or small I am grateful for each and every one of you. Now it's time to pay it forward

1 CHAPTER
WHEN PEOPLE DON'T LISTEN

Most of us can relate to someone in our lives that is always focused on what we've done in the past and chooses not to listen to us in the present moment.

Friends, family, co-workers, and lovers can get stuck in who we used to be, instead of who we are today, they would like to talk and be heard, but rarely do they want to hear us out.

Some of them try to keep us in a place that no longer exists. The past doesn't exist, but of course they keep their record of wrongs, and remind of us the disappointments and failure.

The moment is really the only constructive place for us to be. What was done 8 years ago really cannot be changed, nor does it have a hold on us today in the present.

We have to set boundaries with people and help them understand if they would like to live in the past they have the right to, but we are no longer presently living there.

We also can remind them we choose not to be

reminded about it or criticized about it. If they choose to not listen to us, we surely don't have to listen to them. It works both ways. In effective listening we accept other people for who they are, not who we would like them to be.

Whatever way they live their lives, is their own choice and the lifestyle, and how they have chosen to live.

It is not our purpose or journey to live the life they have chosen. We are separate from them, with our own goals, dreams, and plans in life. We can respect each others dreams and goals. We can learn to accept our differences and walk in harmony.

We could start to realize that our lives belong to us, not someone else's to dictate, or direct for us. We have the right and freedom to choose what is best for us.

We do have the right financially, emotionally, spiritually, and physically to choose what is healthy for us.

If someone chooses to force their opinions and beliefs on us, they should understand they are stepping out of their boundaries.

We sometimes run into those that would like to control the situation or outcome of our lives. They have no control or power over the outcome, only we do.

People have a tendency of being negative towards us, look at the past, and insinuate because we have failed in the past than in the future we will as well.

This is not the truth. We have the ability to turn things around right now. We can change our errors and ways. Plenty of people do every day.

Some people will just choose to knock down every idea you have about your dreams of succeeding. They don't have a tendency to believe the best in you.

Fortunately, many people have to understand what other people have to say doesn't have to have an emotional effect on them, or have to tear their hopes and dreams down.

We just usually have to put them in their place and help them realize they can choose to be positive in our lives, create something good, share something we can both learn and grow from, or they can choose to walk away until they are able to do so.

We can explain at this point in time we don't choose to participate in their negativity. We don't have to participate in it, we don't have to be a part of the negativity.

It doesn't mean we don't love them, but it forces them to respect our boundaries. If we choose to be happy individuals than it is making the right choices to participate in conversations that are healthy and positive for us.

2 CHAPTER
COMMUNICATE YOUR EMOTIONS & FEELINGS

One of the best ways to heal is sharing your story. Everyone has a story. Everyone has had experiences that were traumatic, hurtful, harmful, as well as many triumphs and victories in life.

Express those moments with a group, write your feelings out in a journal, or write a blog about your life experiences. You will learn, you are not alone.

By facing those periods of your life you allow the walls to come down. You will learn to heal in those sensitive areas of your life.

We build up walls because we have been hurt so many times. We lose trust in other people. We feel alone and sometimes we don't believe people understand us.

By reaching out to others even in a blog, we find that we are not so different than other people. We find out we don't have so many differences. We find out we are very connected and more the same in the way we feel about ourselves and other people.

We can feel lonely whether we are around other

people, or even when we isolate ourselves from people. We want to protect ourselves from getting hurt.

We are afraid to tear the walls down. When we build those walls up around us we close out everyone from our lives. We close ourselves in, by not allowing others to come into our sphere.

We can end up living lonely lives if we never allow anyone in, or really dig down deep inside and clear out all the negative feelings and emotions. If we tear those walls down, it helps us find healthy relationships where we can thrive and blossom.

Sometimes we have to risk being ourselves and showing our true feelings and emotions. Once we've faced the fears, we are able to see that everything that once hurt us, doesn't anymore.

We can be truly free of the past if we express how we felt, and feel the emotions. Part of this is grieving over the way we were never loved, how we were never nurtured, how we were never hugged, appreciated, or respected as an individual person.

Many times people will disappoint us, and they will let us down. There are no perfect relationships, and we will always mess up. The biggest lesson is learning to forgive and reconcile our differences.

Forgiveness can take time, it takes time to grieve and heal. It doesn't happen overnight, and it may take several months or years. Everyone heals at different paces, and we just have to give ourselves and other people time to heal and forgive.

Expressing your emotions and feelings and writing them or communicating them to a group can be very therapeutic and healing while at the same time build relationships, and we learn positive ways to cope with our feelings and emotions in a safe environment.

3 CHAPTER
SELF-WORTH

Most of the time in relationships we are seeking love outside of ourselves from another person. We forget that love has to come from our inner self.

We do seek approval and validation from others, but fortunately until we believe we are lovable human beings we will never grasp the idea of our self-worth without ever looking to others to give us this validation.

We live in a world where people are hurting. Hurting people hurt other people verbally, physically, emotionally, and spiritually. We often feel weak, and fall into victimhood without being aware of it.

We find ourselves in power struggles with other people trying to get them to love us, or seek attention in negative ways to get someone to tell us they love us. Of course, when we choose negative behaviors and patterns we push others away, and cause more conflict and distress.

We want things to change, and so we blame others for not changing into the people we would like them to be. We do try to control the situation, try to control them by manipulating them, and playing mind games. We even fall into fear and believe in the worst outcome.

It is not always the truth, and sometimes and illusion. We create our own stories and scenarios with our thoughts about another person hoping we are correct. It's not always the truth. Without hearing it from someone else's mouth, how they feel or think about us, we could be deceiving ourselves.

We can write about any story we want to about our life circumstances, or about the people in our lives. Sometimes we are right when people victimize us by the actions they take.

They may take money, they may take materialism. They may take our heart and break it. I think when we find ourselves in these situations we have to ask ourselves why we choose the relationships that we choose in the first place.

Most of the time it is because we have learned it from generations of dysfunction in our families. We have picked up certain behavior problems, ways of communication, and belief systems that do not teach us how to have healthy relationships.

It is our choice if we want to continue on with the generational dysfunctions and addictions or walk out of being the victim and becoming a survivor.

We can blame it on someone else for our choices and circumstances, but we need to take 100% responsibility in the fact we have created our own story in the moment by the choices we have made.

Whether they are good or bad choices doesn't matter now. In this moment it is more important to learn to make better and healthier choices for our lives.

How do we make better choices? We seek healthy individuals that can teach us better ways to live.

There are many negative people in our lives and naysayers. Whether they are negative or not doesn't really matter. It comes down to a choice of learning our self-worth.

We have to learn to focus on the positive aspects of ourselves. We have to look for the talents and gifts we have deep down within ourselves.

We also need to learn to set boundaries with other people and never allow them to victimize us.

We need to learn to let go of the past realizing it is no longer here.

The past no longer exits. The past doesn't define us. The past doesn't define who we are in the moment or the future.

Who you used to be is not who you are today. At the same time the person in front of you is not the same person as they were yesterday.

We often do have to let go of the past dreams, illusions, fears, and belief systems we held on to for most of our lives that held us back.

Change in our lives is always good. It may be out of our comfort zone. It may be something we're not used too. It does bring up emotions, feelings, and the pain and suffering does have to be surfaced.

In order for you to heal and let go of the negativity from the past; allow it to leave your system once and for all.

Being out of your comfort zone is necessary temporarily. A licensed psychiatrist or psychologist can help you process some of these harsh emotions and feelings if you are having a difficult time.

We cling to pain and suffering because it is familiar, it is something we have learned to do to cope through traumatic experiences as a young child. Although it served us at one point, it is no longer appropriate for us to hang on to it?

We deserve to love ourselves and have healthy relationships. It is a choice of course, and we have the free will to hold on to the old, or transform, and be reborn into a new person.

It is always a choice for us to be a victim of life or a survivor. It is up to us to make our minds strong.

We can hold on to unhealthy relationships and be miserable, or move on to better ones that are healthy and show unconditional love.

The choice is always ours every minute of every day. What is it that you want in your life? You have the choice and there is no excuse that can hold you back from truly having what you want out of life.

The other question is? How bad do you want it? Of course, sometimes it takes a lot of hard work and determination. Pain is temporary, and molds our character. Sometimes we do need to be stretched, and walk out of the comfort zone to become our best selves.

4 CHAPTER
PAIN & SUFFERING

If you are full of pain and suffering most likely you have to make a choice to go on living the way you have always lived or decide to help yourself.

We are either participating in abusive relationships or being abusive towards our self because we are surrounding ourselves with abusive situations.

We are going around in circles abusing others out of our own pain and suffering, as they are abusing us out of their pain and suffering.

We are caught up in the victim mentality. We play the role of victimizing another person, ourselves, or playing the role of the victim.

How do you get out of this? Choosing to stop playing the victim. Take responsibility for your own emotions and feelings. Take responsibility for your own life.

We tend to blame someone else for the outcome of our lives. We blame it on someone else for all our own choices and beliefs.

We can blame it on negativity, we can blame it on other people or make it about good or evil.

Fortunately, these are just excuses why we don't take control over our own lives, and choices.

In the middle of pain and suffering our mind is cloudy and confused. We can't see clearly, and of course bombarding ourselves with negativity.

We have to take responsibility for our lives and admit we are the only ones that are choosing to stay in the frame of mind we are in, in the moment.

We are also the only one's choosing to stay in abusive relationships, and we are the only one's not learning to set emotional, spiritual, and physical boundaries with people.

We are the only ones that are responsible for choosing to hold on to the pain and suffering through emotional, physical, and spiritual attachments.

We choose to cling to emotional and spiritual darkness, or leave it and choose a healthier way of living.

We learn to make the same choices and go

around in circles, or find new ways of coping with our feelings, and emotions.

If you can't take it anymore, perhaps you need to start a new journey in life and find the courage to start helping yourself make better choices.

It takes a few years to sift through your past issues, emotional and spiritual traumas. It takes that time too really get to the root of the problem, learn to set boundaries, how to protect yourself, how to build your mind strong, and change your belief patterns, find your self-worth, find your purpose.

It is a long journey at times discovering who you truly are, and what a beautiful creature you may be. It takes time, devotion, and dedication to yourself to lift yourself up and into higher mindset.

There is no simple solution, no magic potion, only you choosing to make a turnaround in your life by dropping addictions, belief patterns, emotional patterns, and mastering the life lessons you may want to avoid learning with other people.

You have to at some point stop looking outside of yourself for approval from others, and start searching for the answers inside of yourself. While it is work, there is a time when you are free of the clutter and chatter you let loose.

Learn to quiet your thoughts. Learn to stay still for a moment. Learn to let go of all the negative thoughts and feedback from yourself and the world.

Learn to enjoy the beauty of nature, positive relationships, and a world that doesn't seem so dark and gloomy anymore.

There is hope for a better future. There is a better way of learning. You just have to find the courage inside and be brave enough to walk out of the past, and into a better world.

If you have severe depression, grief, or pain and suffering from mental health disorders it's imperative that you ask assistance from a licensed professional such as psychiatrist, psychologist, or therapist in your local area.

When you take the first step to help yourself, problems can be resolved, and solutions can be found.

5 CHAPTER
FINANCIAL PROBLEMS

Many people are struggling financially, have lost homes to foreclosure, have found themselves living in homeless shelters, and standing in lines and human services or non-profits for help.

These are harsh times for many struggling families and know, you are not alone. At the same time you've made choices that have led you to this place, or there has been a death, or divorce. There are many reasons why people can be in situational poverty.

First off the best thing you can do is get new training, education, or experience. Always keep a job, or volunteer somewhere to show that you have been doing something even when you haven't been working.

Visit your local workforce and get instruction on creating and updating your resume and practice your interview skills. Also see if they have funds to help you with training or education to further your job qualifications.

While you may get frustrated filling out multiple applications, this is a whole different experience today than it was back in the 1990's. You need to know how to answer questions in interviews, have the skills, and learn how to stand out from the crowd.

This experience might be over a year, or few years, and you will get tired and want to quit and give up on your job search.

Second, search for a mentor in your area that will encourage you to succeed, that is positive, uplifting, and will push you to move out of your comfort zone. Having a positive person in your life to cheer for you or coach you on your job search, and support you emotionally will get you ahead.

The lesson here is to become confident in yourself, believe in yourself, and challenge yourself to be the best person you can be in the moment.

Find out what you really want to do in life, what your purpose is in life, and what is your passion?

The lesson also is you may be rejected 100 times, but do you allow this to eat away at your self-esteem, or judge yourself by comparing yourself to others?

Are you negative self-talking to yourself through

every step of the way? Are you listening to others tell you what a failure you are? Let me tell you, your negativity, your frown, your anger, your frustration, your stress shows up when you're interviewing.

Learn how to handle your stress, keep a positive mind every day, and learn never to quit, or give up in those moments you do want too. Perhaps the situation is showing you what you're made of, and what you can survive, and what obstacles you can move through, and you never thought you could.

You are being shaped, molded, stretched, and challenged to be a better person, and choose a better life.

You are being tested on what really matters, is it family, materialism, or money? What is true happiness? How much are you worth? How do you see your successes and failures?

The lessons are endless, and of course you can get all depressed and down on yourself, but you won't get hired with self-pity, or feeling sorry for yourself.

So the debt is high, the losses are great, and it hurts emotionally because you are attached to having materialism and money. While these things are nice to have, and of course we all like to have them, this is the question, do you need them to be happy and have a satisfying life?

It is very difficult to lose everything material wise, as well as not have enough money to put food on the table or keep shelter over your head, but you have to take your focus off the problem, and put your focus on how to solve the problem.

What can you do to move out of the situation, and forget what happen in the past? What can you do today, right now to prepare for a better tomorrow?

You can get rid of addictions. They cost money, bad for your health, and relationships. You can get better training or education. You can look for sources online that can help you find a new path.

There are lots of open source educational tools available online. You can work every day on your leadership skills, social skills, writing skills, and much more. There are many resources in your community that can help you as well.

Instead of being frustrated, do something every day to build a better future.

6 CHAPTER
FIND A POSITIVE MENTOR

Find a positive mentor in your life that accepts you and respects you as a human being. It is a true blessing and wonderful thing.

Find one that never gives up on you, and teaches you to fly and soar in life. Mentors encourage you to keep your mind strong and never waver in fear, it's a strength to have the gift to love unconditionally and teach someone to love themselves.

The best gift you can give someone is themselves. It's imperative to find one that is patient and waits for you to learn your life lessons.

It is also important to have a mentor that never judges you or criticizes you in a negative way, and who always believes in the best outcome.

It's a wonderful to have a mentor and teacher to teach you to value yourself and others. Good mentor's never cross their emotional, spiritual, physical, and mental boundaries.

They freely give from a heart filled with passion and a compassion. The best teachers are the ones that have been there themselves and walked the roughest roads.

It doesn't matter what you've done wrong, God forgives you for everything. He never expects you to feel guilty for who he has created you to be.

There are teachers that do take the steps to learn everything themselves, and teach the world to be better people.

When you find one, you have found a treasure. They will walk with you to the end of your journey and be the one who instills confidence in your soul.

They've done their work themselves, and give of their heart without selfishness, greed, or expecting anything in return.

If you're in a bad situation always remember there are people in the world that will believe in you, up lift you, change your life, and teach you to be the best in life.

There are so many out there around the world, and never be afraid to trust the best of them in the world. There is hope, and you just have to have faith, and not allow others to break you down emotionally, mentally, spiritually, or physically.

One day you will be free of pain and suffering and God will heal your soul. Never doubt it, and always have faith in yourself that you can overcome any obstacle.

It doesn't matter what others do in your life, you deserve to value yourself, be loved by a healthy family, and have a healthy marriage, healthy children, and love is never a fight.

Rely on God's love. Always put a hedge of protection around your children and family with prayer.

Know God will always protect you and pave the way regardless of others interference and bad choices.

Life can be hard and cruel, but you have the inner strength to fly and soar and be free of shackles and chains of generations of addictions, abuse, and other bad habits, beliefs, and behaviors.

True happiness can be found even in the middle of a raging storm. Just always fill your heart with love and be faithful to God.

Keep your heart open wide, and allow God's love to heal it every day. Fill your mind and soul with positive things, nurturing your soul and spirit every day.

What others choose to do in your life is not your fault, and never blame yourself, or carry the burden. All you can do is your best to be your best self.

Eventually you will move out of the storm and reach sunshine and feel the rays of God's healing love. It may take a lot of work, but it can happen.

You are always in control in the moment of what happens to you, every thought, every action, and every belief. Other's stories and beliefs about you are not yours.

The past has nothing to do with the present, and staying in the now, this moment you have the tools and instrument to build a beautiful future. One day at a time and one moment at a time.

Hold on tight to God's love and always forgive others and let it go. People don't mean to harm you, and you must always have compassion for those who harm you. Send them love and say a prayer every day. Wait patiently for God to move in their lives.

7 CHAPTER
WHY IS YOUR LIFE THE WAY IT IS?

Why is your life the way it is? Our life becomes old, but we have created our life. We cannot escape the life we have created.

We have acted a certain way to get here. We don't think about what we have done yesterday, in our childhood, or even last year.

Whatever we did had a cause and effect. There are consequences to every behavior and action.

We do suffer in our lives. We create our own suffering for ourselves or others. We say things, do things, and we are usually hurting ourselves and others.

We fill our own world with suffering.

We end up creating our happy life or miserable life. We can be kind to others, or hateful. We can be jealous or envious.

We can wish ill-feelings and ill-health on others. Everything has a cause and effect and of course it does affect our lives emotionally, spiritually, physically, and mentally.

Our mindset determines the outcome of our reality in the present moment and how we act towards another human being or animal.

We decide where to take our lives, and how to handle our relationships with other people.

We cannot ignore the effect we have on another person financially, emotionally, spiritually, mentally, or physically.

We can inflict suffering, or hold back and ease other people's suffering. We are all related and connected. We cannot exist without touching another soul in a positive or negative way.

We have to have compassion and understanding. Perhaps even slip on someone else's shoes and try to imagine what it would be like to experience what they do in life.

We don't have control over other people's intentions. We don't have control over how they think or feel. We have no control over their actions.

Future suffering is just the result of the suffering we have caused in the past towards ourselves or another person.

Suffering can only create more suffering. We have to take responsibility of our actions, how we respond, and react in other people's life.

In time we can heal and become our best selves. We can focus on giving love and healing the hearts of others, or keep inflicting pain.

We have to neutralize the negative feelings, and replace them with positive ones.

We need to take control of our thoughts. We need to take control of our actions and feelings. We need to do what is for the highest good of our own selves and others around us.

Love is really the only answer. The act of kindness can change a heart. We can do great things in the world instead of accepting we all have to live and suffer.

We don't have to live in suffering.
We choose to live in suffering by making up excuses, playing the victim, and thinking we are helpless and not setting boundaries with others.

We are not helpless, and we are the only ones that can change the path and direction of our lives. Why would you want to put your life in someone else's hands and expect them to save you?

What if they do lead you down the wrong path? What if they do give you the wrong answers? What if your life ends upside down, because you failed to understand you have the personal power to be something more, and create your own life?

Why blame it on someone else for you not living the life you want too?

We do make all the choices, and we do have to take responsibility for the outcome. We create our own suffering by holding certain beliefs, thoughts, and feelings.

We move in circles and don't learn our lessons, and we fail to see the only one that can change our lives around is ourselves every moment.

Instead we fall victim to the darkness instead of remaining in the light and love. Love is always the way out of darkness. When we focus on the beautiful things in ourselves and others we can see their true divine nature.

8 CHAPTER
SAVE ME

Most of us have a lot of pain and suffering buried deep down inside. We stuff away our traumatic experiences in our personal suitcase, burying them in the bottom of the closet, perhaps the drawer, and hope we never have to look back.

Wrong! If we don't face our fears, we bring our luggage with us in to the next relationship whether it is friendship, family, work, or lovers. We end up making a bigger disaster out of our lives.

We can even drink and get high hoping that will make it go away. We can have sex with a lot of people, and only find ourselves hurt again and again.

We can switch friends, partners, even leave our family, hoping this will solve the problem. Maybe we can even gamble all our money away.

Fortunately nothing every resolves the empty feeling inside. Nothing takes away the loneliness, and nothing makes you feel better.

Why? You have to take responsibility for your

life. There is no way out of it. You can run as fast as you can away from everything packed in that suitcase, but eventually it comes back around unless you face it head on.

It may be painful, it may hurt, and you may even cry. The problem is stuffing it away for safe keeping and hoping it never shows itself, well it's not realistic.

That pain and suffering is in your body, your thoughts, and your spirit. It comes out on your face, whether you can smile or not. It can come out in the way you speak.

Vulgar words, or loving words you get to pick. It comes out in the way you see things. What you believe, perceive, and how you form your opinions.

It comes out in your actions whether you are aggressive, or gentle in your approach with other people. It comes out in how you communicate.

When you're in a loving relationship, you have a hard time letting go of them when they break up with you because you don't want to let go. You need them to feel good about yourself.

You need them to tell you, you are okay,

beautiful, smart, funny, or whatever. You feel they need to verify the way you feeling inside. If they're not there, who's going to save you from yourself?

Who's going to stop you from telling yourself how well or bad you are? Who is going to tell you that you don't have to be guilty or shameful for being who you are in the moment?

Who is going to tell you that you are forgiven for making mistakes? There are a million conversations you have with yourself over your past and future.

You beat yourself up and use other people to make yourself feel better. Other people are not going to make you feel better all the time.

It is nice to get compliments. It is nice to feel loved. It is nice to be in a relationship. We just have a tendency to hurt other people because we are hurting ourselves.

While you may be filled with a lot of pain and suffering the reason why relationships don't work out is because you are filled with too much anger, hurt, resentment, bitterness, and don't really understand yourself.

You often wonder why you are in this place. It's

everyone else's fault why your life is the way it is. You take no responsibility for what you have created yourself. You build up walls and protect yourself so you won't get hurt again. Which is understandable.

At some point you cannot feel love unless you open up your heart and allow other people in to help you. While people may have hurt you in the past, they are not here today, and can no longer hurt you the way they did.

After you've hurt yourself enough times, you will hit rock bottom. You may have lost everything from finances, relationships, materialism, and a home, but at some point you have to go through all that luggage, and determine what to do with it.

Unpack it, sort through it and take a look at it, and ask yourself why you are so afraid of it?

Whatever is in the past can't hurt you anymore. Forgive those people, let it go, and release it. Don't hold on to it. Let it go. The only one that can truly save you in life is you.

9 CHAPTER
SAVE ME

Most of us have a lot of pain and suffering buried deep down inside. We stuff away our traumatic experiences in our personal suitcase, burying them in the bottom of the closet, perhaps the drawer, and hope we never have to look back.

Wrong! If we don't face our fears, we bring our luggage with us in to the next relationship whether it is friendship, family, work, or lovers. We end up making a bigger disaster out of our lives.

We can even drink and get high hoping that will make it go away. We can have sex with a lot of people, and only find ourselves hurt again and again.

We can switch friends, partners, even leave our family, hoping this will solve the problem. Maybe we can even gamble all our money away.

Fortunately nothing every resolves the empty feeling inside. Nothing takes away the loneliness, and nothing makes you feel better.

Why? You have to take responsibility for your life.

There is no way out of it. You can run as fast as you can away from everything packed in that suitcase, but eventually it comes back around unless you face it head on.

It may be painful, it may hurt, and you may even cry. The problem is stuffing it away for safe keeping and hoping it never shows itself, well it's not realistic.

That pain and suffering is in your body, your thoughts, and your spirit. It comes out on your face, whether you can smile or not. It can come out in the way you speak.

Vulgar words, or loving words you get to pick. It comes out in the way you see things. What you believe, perceive, and how you form your opinions.

It comes out in your actions whether you are aggressive, or gentle in your approach with other people. It comes out in how you communicate.

When you're in a loving relationship, you have a hard time letting go of them when they break up with you because you don't want to let go. You need them to feel good about yourself.

You need them to tell you, you are okay, beautiful,

smart, funny, or whatever. You feel they need to verify the way you feeling inside. If they're not there, who's going to save you from yourself?

Who's going to stop you from telling yourself how well or bad you are? Who is going to tell you that you don't have to be guilty or shameful for being who you are in the moment?

Who is going to tell you that you are forgiven for making mistakes? There are a million conversations you have with yourself over your past and future.

You beat yourself up and use other people to make yourself feel better. Other people are not going to make you feel better all the time.

It is nice to get compliments. It is nice to feel loved. It is nice to be in a relationship. We just have a tendency to hurt other people because we are hurting ourselves.

While you may be filled with a lot of pain and suffering the reason why relationships don't work out is because you are filled with too much anger, hurt, resentment, bitterness, and don't really understand yourself.

You often wonder why you are in this place. It's

everyone else's fault why your life is the way it is. You take no responsibility for what you have created yourself. You build up walls and protect yourself so you won't get hurt again. Which is understandable.

At some point you cannot feel love unless you open up your heart and allow other people in to help you. While people may have hurt you in the past, they are not here today, and can no longer hurt you the way they did.

After you've hurt yourself enough times, you will hit rock bottom. You may have lost everything from finances, relationships, materialism, and a home, but at some point you have to go through all that luggage, and determine what to do with it.

Unpack it, sort through it and take a look at it, and ask yourself why you are so afraid of it?

Whatever is in the past can't hurt you anymore. Forgive those people, let it go, and release it. Don't hold on to it. Let it go. The only one that can truly save you in life is you.

10 CHAPTER
STANDING IN THE SPOTLIGHT

If you can imagine a spotlight coming from heaven following you wherever you go on earth, under this spotlight is where you are being your best self.

This is where you are being a supportive partner, daughter, wife, sister, brother, son, father, or friend. This is when you are kind hearted filled with compassion and empathy for other people.

This is when you are loving towards others whether they are being harmful or hurtful to you. In the spotlight you speak calmly without fear or intimidation. You have a positive mind, see the best in others and believe in the best at all times.

When you step out of the spotlight you can guarantee you're in the darkness. You are insulting, intimidating, controlling, manipulating, hurtful, and angry, frustrated, and attack others for every short coming and fault.

You use violence some times to get your way. Maybe even use drugs, alcohol, gambling, pornography, or other means of substance abuse, or addictions. This is your worst self.

When you have one foot in the spot light and one foot in the darkness you are going back and forth between polarities.

You are in chaos and confusion, doubt, fear, and may not make the best choices. You haven't quite figured out how to speak calmly, and get caught in other people's insults, and arguments.

You are balanced some times, and other times you are off balance trying to master your life lessons in communicating verbally, emotionally, physically, and spiritually.

When you have conquered the lessons in life you are balanced and a whole person. You have no need to step out of the spotlight and into the darkness. You have no need to argue.

You have no need to be harmful to yourself or others. You are loving towards yourself, animals, plant life, and the earthly environment that surrounds you. You don't need to kill anything whether it's someone emotionally, or take it out on any living breathing thing.

When you learn to conquer your own life lessons and can walk in your spotlight all the time alone, without depending on anyone else, you are independent and free of the past.

You can let go of it, and you can understand it has no place in the present moment. You have no need to bring it up. You have no need to use it against another human being.

If we look at this for a moment as a wound on our flesh it will heal over time. When someone comes along and brings the past up it is like them taking a scalpel on your flesh and cutting it open.

When we do it is exposing the wound again so it will not stay shut. If it is in the process of healing we are peeling off the scab so it will never continue to heal.

Fortunately, we do this a lot in our society and wonder why no one is getting better or healed. We fail to see all the positive things a person is doing.

Someone can be desperately trying to make the changes in their lives, and it takes time, patience, understanding and empathy.

If you don't have the patience or any of the above these are the lessons you need to learn and achieve. Not only with others but with yourself as well. When you feel someone else needs to change, this is when it is you that needs to change.

It is when you need to take a good look in the mirror and understand you're in the same place as them. There is no blaming or excuses. You have both co-created the scenario together to learn certain lessons and mirror each other.

You may be at the opposite ends of the spectrum and have two different life styles, but you have to learn to live with the differences and understand you're both right. You're both wrong. You have to be team players and discuss what the positive solutions are, and not be stubborn and just have your own way all the time.

It may take some time to stand in the spotlight at all times, but one moment at a time, one second at a time we do reach that place. It is a lot of work, and fortunately without doing the work or changing ourselves we will never see the results we want to in life.

Love is not negative. It is not hurtful or harmful to others. It always has everyone's best interest in mind. It will always seek out positive and give up lifting solutions.

The whole key is getting yourself in this spotlight at all times, and when you have achieved this there will be others who walk in your life and be in alignment with you who are healthier.

You will have the appropriate people surrounding your life, and the job that is appropriate for you.

You are doing what is appropriate for you and letting go of all the things that are not appropriate for you anymore. You are always becoming your best self.

Evaluate whether you're in this spotlight from heaven every day. You can see and monitor your progress and see what you need to work on. It may take some time. If you have patience with yourself than you will have patience for others.

If you have empathy for yourself than you will for others. If you have forgiveness for yourself you will have it for others. When you can love you and be your best self, than you allow others to do the same.

You are also able to have compassion and empathize with others. You end up loving others unconditionally without harming yourself or them in the process.

When you feel good about who you are, you can feel good about the world and other people in your life.

HATTIE SPIRITWEAVER

www.ingramcontent.com/pod-product-compliance
Lightning Source LLC
Chambersburg PA
CBHW030542290526
45786CB00004B/1818